And Then It Hit Me

Derek Welch

BookLeaf Publishing

India | USA | UK

Presentation by *BookLeaf Publishing*

Web: www.bookleafpub.com

E-mail: info@bookleafpub.com

ISBN: 9789360940447

First edition 2024

Choosing to be here.

PREFACE

I didn't know what I would see,
I didn't know how much it would matter;
But the answer to both happened to be,
"So much more than I expected"

Pulse

I shuffled the door to the right so it would latch,
Walked down the uneven steps and took a left.

Cold night tonight - brisk with breath in the air;
A shiver followed by a chin tuck into my coat -
Cold, but not terrible.

I'm not stupid,
I've noticed the crossroads to my vice has a
blinking red light in the middle of it.
It's slow monotone red repeating:
Stop. Stop. Stop.

Groaning:
Slow down. Look around you. Take it in;
Think.

Yet just behind it is a sign surrounded by a
dancing green flash;
It says: I'm Open;
Quick - come here! You've still got time.

I'm not dumb, but I do wonder if I'm weak.

Once inside, muscle memory leads me to the 4th
cooler from the left -

Strong beer with low price tags.
Fancy ones from fancy places that sound better
when you say how much you like them.

Now, normally I reserve this trip for nights of
relaxation.
Or nights when I have heavy stress on my mind,
Or nights when I'm bored;
Lonely, Happy, Horny, Alive.

But tonight I made an exception. I'm working on
something I care about, you see;
It can be hard.

So, with my motivation intact, I walk to the
cashier whose own muscle memory has my price
on the screen before I get there,
I pay my dues and get my change - 50 cents;
Maybe more importantly - 2 quarters.

I say importantly because to the exit is waiting a
game - I'll be brief because I feel like you'll
know what I mean.

Simple Rules: Put a quarter in the slot: see if a
steel wall pushes it against other quarters. Hope
that it does - and hope that it pushes more
quarters down a little hole that lets you have
them.

It's a game I've been playing since childhood
casinos with the mouse mascot;
I've been trained for this.

I make my way up, seeing that it was primed -
fully loaded. Quarters teased the edge, saying
"Oh, it could be you. Oh, it should be you. Oh,
no yes, it's going to be you"

I walked up and heard, "Let me get a shot first
my man".

I turn to see - this was the first break in my
pattern and I'm used to blindly following my
habits -

I see another man sporting the same paper bag as
me. Looking just as chilled by the night,
And I become instantly sure that our reasons for
being here are nearly the same.

"We can take turns?"
"Sure, sure"

He slipped his quarter into the slot, a solid push
but no movement.
"Close!"

Another coin slipped from his fingers into the
machine.

The monotonous groan of it moved his change
into the middle of a thousand changes that no
longer move.

"Shit, you go"

I asked where to aim. He pointed, excitedly.

My quarter had the New River Gorge Bridge on
the back of it,
I noticed as gave it away.

A decent movement, one of the few five-dollar
bills had inched closer to being mine;
My heart beat faster. I told him this.

"Hit it again man, it's so close, same spot"

I did.

Nothing. Not even a slight nudge or tease. Cold,
like machines like this usually are;
Uncaring that I had given it Connecticut's oak
tree as tribute.

The man left without any words -as they seem to
do;
A few heart-flushed moments suffice for most of
us.

I followed, stepping out of the little shop I know
too well.

Looking up,
It was as if my smokey breath was holding that
lights familiar pulsing red:

Stop.
Stop.
stop.

Think.

Gram At Christmas

Gentle laughs as I hold shaky hands -
They're so soft.
I suppose it makes sense - weathered smooth by
70 years of touching hearts;

Holding child, grandchild, and great:
Cousin, nephew, friend, daughter, sibling -
family.
These hands have rubbed across the backs of the
most important types of people.

And tonight, I'm holding them next to a
Christmas tree.

I had been watching you - with your Santa outfit
and teary eyes.
Watching the way you were watching us - eyes
holding a feeling that no words could fit;
Straining to take in every detail of a full living
room -
Enjoying the gentle waves of, "My babies are
here; all of my babies are here".

It was the first time in a while I noticed you
were wearing your old, small smile;
The one you had gotten when you first became a
mother -
You've always worn it beautifully.
For as long as I can remember, it's suited you.

I sit next to you on the footstool.
You look toward me without us needing to
speak;
We lock eyes and, for a moment, all the words
we didn't have filled our hearts at the same time
-
Leaving our chests as small exhales through
gentle smiles:

"I love you, Gram"
"I know baby. I love you too"

All that studying

I've studied the stars - their shapes & stories;
Learned the names of the planets who weave
and wave between them.

I've read about the retrogrades and
manifestations,
The Secret & King James -
Witnessed Jehova; Ganesha's Sharanam.

Archetypes, prototypes, Myers & Briggs;
Running my fingers over the maps of internal
language the world around me uses -
Tinkering with ancient compasses who claim
their own True North.

9 numbers, 12 signs, 4 seasons, 66 books, 81
verses;
Days, weeks, years -
Knowing even these could only ever be half-torn
library pages.

Psychology meets patterns meets mythology
meets biology;
My ears turn to fine-tuned instruments when
they speak

Measuring word, inflection, and background;
Keeping tally of body language, aura, and the
slant in their eyes -
"Oh yes, I know what you're saying"

I call myself a mirror, but perhaps I'm more akin
to a collection of Scrabble pieces:
All the worlds and words waiting to be found,
claimed, announced.

It does leave me to wonder,
With over four thousand names and words and
faces and places;
Scriptures, oracles, prophets, and sage:

How do I speak my world simply?

I grow anxious that I'll be left speaking in a
language no one else has tried to discover;
Fearful of the isolation of being a universal
validation donor.

But my truth's north has led me to others who
walk in the same direction through their own
means.
Meeting folk with their own distinct accents that
remind me of a part of home I cannot call mine,
But smells like lilac all the same.

Maybe the truth is more akin to smell than
language?
A gentle waft of memory and feeling;
Wordless with a million words to try and
explain.

And, rather than using words we try to call Holy
to explain;
Maybe the truth shows up best when we do.

A Purr

11

Simple things that you know you want -
Do I use the phrase, "know you deserve"?;
Demand you get?
Cats are weird, but I like cuddling with you too.

Reboot

I didn't expect to live to see the sequel.
The new thing is to call it the next chapter, but
the sentiment is the same;
After 30 years you kind of give up seeing
anything new -
At least something worthy of keeping your
attention.

The author takes his time, that much is clear -
30 years of this slow build-up of plot points and
character;
It's worth it though - without it, that emotional
punch at the end of last season wouldn't have hit
as hard.

Man that was crazy,
Wasn't it?

The part where that main guy ended up in the
hospital with scabs on his wrist -
Those phone calls to his mom in the middle of
the night? Ugh, truly devastating.
I'm honestly surprised the author chose to keep
the story going -
The twist of him waking up the next morning? I
didn't see that coming.

Then there were those weird spin-off series:
The one where he quit his job. The one where he
almost lost his partner;
The one where he rediscovered God.

I trust that they serve the bigger story, but for a
while there it really felt like the plot was lost.
Maybe it was just me, but it felt hard to follow;
Especially because it felt like the climax had
already happened.

I hope it doesn't end up being one of those series
where the best episodes are at the start -
One of those where we end up agreeing that it
should've died before the reboot.

I do trust the new co-writer though.

He has a few credits on earlier segments; I'm
pretty sure He wrote the Yellowstone Saga -
Vermont and North Carolina too, and a credit in
the meeting of partners.

I'm only a few episodes in, I binged them in a
few months - and there's this subtle change to
the tone I'm excited to see the authors explore
together. It's cute;

I really didn't expect the story to keep going,
But I'm so in love with the character so -

I'm willing to give this new chapter a chance.

Resume

It's strange developing two sides of myself in
tandem -
A piece of the Gemini's Curse?

Derek Welch's Employment Resume
Climbing of ranks, increase in influence,
completing of responsibilities; reasons why you
should pay me more than I've been paid before.

Derek Welch's Passion List
More unfinished songs than finished, chakras
balanced most days, a few speaking events, a
body that smiles more often than it frowns.

Personal vs Professional - is that how I should
say it?
One sellable to a system, one smaller for the
soulful -
Wallet vs Heart? Prestige vs Purpose?

I feel a merge coming along and it feels
counter-intuitive;
As if I've learned to hold my power within the
market rather than my own fruit trees -
But something is changing..

It's saying:

Be proud of your ability to share a product, as
much as I can be proud of the product I produce.
I've become so good at selling other folk's
wares - I wonder if I'm learning the value of my
own.

Personal Philosophy: 1+1=3

3) Derek Welch's Intention
Words that climb through ranks, energy inspiring
positive influence, speaking when asked to
speak - while knowing the significance of doing
so.

1) My Body;
Smiles as it's valued for the fruits of its labor -
the kind its spirit produces.

A Night at the end of the year

Do I write about my mom tonight?
Do I write about my partner -

Do I write about my sister crying,
Do I write about my brother?

It's been an intense few weeks if I'm being
honest with this computer -
Full of the humans I love the most being more
human than normal.

I could never fault them.

My mom, she cried at the thought of not being
enough -
My partner fights a war to prove that he is.

My sister sleeps, comforted by her husband,
My brother wrapped in his first vinyl strings.

Uncles laughing, grandmas clapping -
Cousins dancing, full moon rising;

This Christmas has been honest.

If empathy were to dictate my state, I'd be a
mess;
If feeling what others feel was who I am, I'd feel
much less -

-

Because tonight - right here - witnessing all that
I've seen come to pass;
I feel close to the point of bursting,
Stretched thin by a feeling I'm sure will last.

What do I call myself tonight?

A safe place to start:
Grateful - grateful I've been blessed with people
who are people.
Blessed?; Blessed with stories of heart and
triumph and pain.

Thankful I've learned that I can't fix everything:
Thankful I've learned that my co-dependance
isn't just pain.
;
I can't soothe my mother's tears and my sister's
fears and my boyfriend's worries or my uncle's
years. I can't fix the dog's anger or the
step-mom's wishing;
Nor the hole in the floor, or the snow layer
missing.

I can be here for you through it all though;

I can smile, and dance, and listen, and love.

I can see you here
Christmas bows in your hair;

I can tell you it makes sense,
This all seems unfair -

But part of me will whisper like that part always
does -
"This is all for the better, this is all for true love"

Because love, it seems, doesn't hide nor it boast
-
Love is ourselves, when we hate it the most.

It's that ugly, that foul, that old open wound;
And it's the parts of the other who might just
hug us too soon.
-
I watched healing this year,
In the shape of humans showing up humanly.

I watched honesty burn away past storylines,
And laughs pass by naturally.
-

Part of love is truth, and part of truth is pain,
And what makes all the difference,
Is seeing that it's the same.
-

A thousand thoughts this year;
If not a thousand more.

But I couldn't be more happy,
These are who I adore.

Stretching Latex

A balloon nearly full,
Plastic barrier stretching thin;

I need not dictate the direction,
A new way of being is soon to begin.
-

-

It's a swell leading to stretch marks on my ego,
Small tears in the skin of who I think I am.

My heart a bicycle pump;
Every excited beat adds to the well in my chest -
Every exhale containing more and more of the
things I'm made of.

I'm picking up speed in the ways that you do
when things are nearly done;
Every daydream adding to the water-park-bucket
about to spill over -
The bells are ringing and my inner-child is
rushing to be doused.

Drenched in the echoing "pop" of things fuller
than their manmade limitations.

I am made of water,
I am made of air;

It is in my nature to flow into ever-growing
spaces -
& so I shall.

Mystery

This thing is slow,
This thing is wet,
It's oh-so moist,
It's oh-so fat;

But don't be scared,
He holds no threat,
This here's my frog,
His name is Matt.

Nearly There

A coping mechanism I've picked up from my
ADHD is making a list of things to do,
And then making the best route from A to B to
complete all of my tasks,
And then repeat my to-do list like a mantra until
I go to sleep.

This then this then this then that;
All day I am not where I am, I'm only on the
way to where I'm supposed to be.

At work: this works,
At home: I don't feel at home.

In bed, I'm in tomorrow,
Tomorrow, I'm in bed -
Always 3 steps ahead of wherever I find my
head to be.

It's helpful in the way that "things get done" -
Laundry, bills, cleaned up living room.

But my Spirit gathers dust despite my body
never stopping;
Like the fan in the bedroom -
Life turns to white noise.

I'm trying to slow down, I really am -
But the silence of the moment has grown
intimidating;
Like the world has become an eerie hotel room
on the way out west -
It's hard to calm down into the stillness.

But, after I write this, I'm going to light a
candle,
Get in the shower,
And let the mixing of flame and water calm the
obligation of my motion.

Love you Derek,
This is a new year.

Stirring

I have to assume that my ability to daydream is a gift:

My ability to imagine things beyond where my feet are touching the ground -
Blend complex images and logistics into possibilities;
Seeing whole worlds that may just happen.

Moving them from the realm of dreams to my waking life has been tricky -
I get caught wondering if I'm doing enough or if I know where to start;
Do I know how to begin, do I have what it takes;
It's hard to trust making something if you're the first person to ever do it.

So, for a long time, my gift has been something shiny I keep tucked away except for journals and my R.E.M cycles. A nice thing on the shelf that I enjoy knowing I have -
But I've never really been able to nail down how to use it in a way more than a fleeting way to pass the time.

But it's got this glow lately;
Almost like it's waking up -

And I think it's asking me to do the same.

NYE

I ended the year in a bar I knew was
over-capacity;
Strobe lights and bass-hits rattling both my body
and my neurons.

Flashing faces around me;
Hands hoisting cocktails into the sky,
Bodies smiling and swaying - almost in rhythm.

I was nearing the point of oversaturation;
The rum wasn't strong enough to dilute the feast
of sensation -
The colors and flashes and sounds and people
and bodies and sex;

But I saw my partner there.
His first time out for the new year,
His head back, champagne near his neck;
Eyes closed - body at the DJ's mercy.

So very lost in the feelings of being alive -
Surrounded and comforted by the experience
that can only be called
Queer liberation:

Bodies taught to blend in now dancing: taut in
fishnet;
Hands holding and lips meeting -
Humans laughing at just how human they were
allowing themselves to be.

I saw him,
Soaking in the goosebumps from the subwoofer
-
Wrists folding close as the beat rose quicker;

He opened his eyes and smiled,
Came close;
"Happy New Year,
I Love You"

-

And now I'm here.

Oh, Wait

30

Forgive me,
I had slipped back into my victim mindset there
for a second;

Can we start over?

Cool, thank you,
Now;

Who the fuck did you think you were talking to?

Does the Oak Wonder

My anxiety has found a home in the crook of my
DNA swirls;
The place where crossing patterns meet -
Like a squirrel nesting in the splitting of
branches.

It's a piece of the tree now - family, genetics,
storyline;
It's a part of the story now -
This is just how it's grown.

I do wonder;
Does the Oak ever wonder the questions I
wonder -
Was now the time to change things?

Given time:
Does the Elm question her choices of choosing
branches-
Or is she content with how her nature chose to
chase the sun?

Does the Ash ever wonder -
Did I do it right?

Birch;
Have I done enough?

I know tomorrow's poem will hold that question
more directly,
But I needed a warm-up tonight;
Something to remind me of the forest I'm living
in.

Something that reminds me that nature is a gift -
Mine Included -
And that the nature of nature is much more
forgiving than I am.

Abundance happens in cycles -
Even the gnats know this;
Worm to Wolf -

But here I am:
3 beers deep in a cramped & cozy living room,
Unable to quiet the wondering;

Have I done enough?

Diagnosis

I'm an ugly optimist,
My first therapist told me as much:

"You are hopeful to the point of delusion"
Clinical words from a doctorate man to describe
my early 20's disposition;

I've learned to learn to look for the signs:
I am stronger than I think I am,
I am not as strong as I think I am.

Teaching myself to notice:
Just because you can see the stories in front of
you for the stories they are,
Doesn't mean that you need to watch them as
closely as you do.

Man, if only he had said that instead.

The polluted sense of pleasure that got me
through my early abuse :
"This makes sense, honest"

Aka;
A dedication to the significance of experience -
As painful as it may be;

As long-lasting as its effect may last -

This is a chance to live a life that tells a story;
And the story you tell has the chance to live
beautifully.

It's no wonder that I find myself having a hard
time processing anger;
"Nothing can be ugly if it's all on time"
The long-held understanding.

But now I see that the ugliness is just as on time
as the event that caused it;
Aka;
The range of what you feel is all equally valid.

But I'm still an ugly optimist.

I can't put down this nagging notion that even
the ugliest of feelings are on time -
That even my darkest of days are teaching me
about the brightest of ones to come.

Or ones that have been,
Or ones that I dream of;

It's on time,
Regardless.

I wallow in a self-pity:
The kind of a boy who thinks he sees the whole
story.

I'm working on nuance,
I promise.

But:
What's a boy to do when he finds his clinically
diagnosed superpower is the way things are?

Lol;
Wouldn't it be nice if I knew

Storm in the Kitchen

I cried today while I did the dishes.

It was the whirlwind kind of crying -
Subtle movement of ideas, scraps of paper,
moving in circles;
Rotation mixed with a back and forth.

Then a true gust came from my gut -
The shudders hit the heart(h) so hard that the
blinds no longer worked:

I was looking from the outside in,
Seeing myself again as a small boy with a fear
of the wind -
Fearful of rain;
Forgetful of its importance.

I had placed walls around this part of myself -
Straw & Stick;
Part of me knew that these wouldn't hold -
Part of me never wanted to hide as deeply as I
have.

The slow swirling clouds above me block the
Son,
They whispered in old voices,
"You have let yourself become nothing".

Uninspired, Directionless, Co-dependant;
Finding next direction by asking others what
they'd have you do.

The walls around me tumble in resemblance of
Jericho,
The thunder's voice trumpeting curses at their
foundations -
Shaken by Holy words.

And I am there, naked in the truth of my
long-standing storm;
My voice holds the glow of the sun - despite him
hiding behind rain-filled clouds -
"I am inspired. I am creative. I am guided."

Discontent is motivation to change;
Seed through soil,
My urge to move is a sign that I am alive.

And that sign will be enough;
Just as I am.

The winds sweep through my hair,
The sink begins to overflow;
I smile at the rain dancing down my cheek.

Enough

"Am I doing enough"

I have been plagued by this question for weeks
now and all I keep coming back to is,
"Enough for what?"

Doing enough to make writing my career,
Enough to find inspiration,
Enough play,
Enough to make money,
Enough travel?

Am I making enough time for myself,
Am I doing enough of what makes me happy,
Do I have enough ideas of what that means?

It's this caterpillar eating at the back of my
mind,
Slow bites out of my senses of security -
I fear what it would transform into if I keep
feeding it.

Or am I the one searching for scraps?;
Looking for small pieces that remind me that I
am right where I need to be?

That breathing is enough,
That laughing is enough,
That writing poems for myself is enough -

But oh how I miss those mountains;
The wonder they forced into my heart has
birthed some sort of songbird;

She sings to me all night,
Echoing through my chest like an elk bugling
through Lamar Valley -

My heart holds her cries for beauty,
My mind holds a hunger for more -
Are they destined to meet?
Should I keep them separate for safety's sake?
.

It's the fate of the moth to succumb to a
songbird;
Should I let it happen?

Will that finally be enough?

Heart On My Sleeve

My heart sits a bit too full as I sit it a bit too far
out on my sleeve;
Drops of honesty fall out and pitter onto the
living room floor -
Just a few, but it smells like roses the moment
before they soak into the carpet.

Every word I say shakes my body,
I'm trying to keep it all balanced -
To hold myself together,
But it's gotten a bit out of hand.

It'd be easier to share if I knew what was inside
-
If I knew that it would be roses and sage;
But there's this feeling I can't shake.
Something like: at the end of the cup, there'll be
old coffee grounds I forgot to clean out.

Scab & soot from phoenix flame,
Tar and taint from all those ideas I once believed
about myself.

But this year's holidays have filled my heart to
the point of spilling,
And even my habits of stillness are not enough
to keep it inside.

I will, undoubtedly, speak the right word at the
right time, and the swell of my chest -
Or the catch of my breath will cause composure
to crumple,

My hand will go to my chest,
As it always does when a feeling sneaks through
the mesh I've placed around myself.
The glass will fall,
My heart will break open,
And the sobs will bounce around the room like
ghosts who've forgotten which afterlife they're
destined to.

And the world will smell like lilac, then funeral
incent, then salt and sulfur -
And I will stand soaked in a year's worth of
truths I didn't know I was holding onto.

They soak into the carpet,
They soak into my skin.

I collect the pieces of a heart that's held so
much;

Mending them together with a soft glue made of
"I Love You".

Heart on my sleeve, as always;
Hand on my heart,

We start again.

Chapter Setting

I was there,
Not for all of it, not for the worst -
But that story crossed my horizon and shadowed
me too.

It gave me memories I've only just started to
remember:
Ones that sit just outside of a sober mind -
The ones that say "Flood the brain, let me out -
Smoke me out;
Take anything you have - turn your mind to dust
- forget me finally."

The whisper,
More feeling than word,
"Keep quiet and numb yourself".

I don't know the whole story,
But I know mine touches yours.

I know that you were a savior in confusing
times;
Holding hands and playing games while the
shadows watched and waited.
I know you saved me on that river.

I know you feel alone,
I think it's a side effect of stolen innocence.

I'll say it even though I know you feel it:
I do love you. Very much.

The sun seems to be setting on an over-stayed
chapter;
The shadows grow tall, the stars start to shine -
This is the part of the story where remembering
to look for the little lights is crucial.

But, just like when we were young -
You are not doing this alone.
I am here;
I promise.

Two Rivers

There's a hill I know of that lets you watch two
rivers meet;

One coming down from the north in a slow
meander,
The other coming from the south - having just
finished a tour through rapid.

They meet just east of a crossroads, despite their
different backstories.
And when they do,
There's no slamming of waters when they touch.

It's something near watching a basket be made
of sweet grass,
Currents weaving in and out of each other,
Bobbing and dipping in little ripples of
nearly-waves -
And then, with joint consensus, the river moves
west.

The snow-filled north holds hands with the rapid
charged south,
Together they slowly flow west.

This is the part of the river that sustains life;
Bear, moose, elk, me on hard days.
Together they become expansive, and deep, and
nourishing -

But I know of another hill.
From there I can watch the river split ways - one
continuing west, the other north.
One joins a lake - I've never seen where the
other goes.

When I think of the story, it all makes sense.
The meeting, flowing, producing, departing.
Forever carrying some of the water from the
other -
Or maybe it's forever changed;
Not one or another, but something new entirely.

I wonder if someone is on a hill watching me as
I meet the people I love.
Watching how we come together from rapid and
rain -
How we grow deeper, nourishing the lives
around us -
Then one day we part.

Forever changed by a meeting long carved into
stone.

The Last Poem

The last poem of the book:
I'm tempted to use an old one that I know packs
a punch -
But who am I trying to impress?

Of course, I want to go out with a bang,
But I want it to be one that I earned,
You know?

I want it to be true -
To know I can do this, and I did.

To see, in ink, that I can sit and hold my day
with an honest heart-
And I can try and attach ransom-letter stickers to
it in a way that reminds me of its value.

My days had a habit of going by me without
much notice,
Routine robs me of insight.
I imagine that a room full of Van Gogh does the
same eventually -
Honest and lovely beautiful things can seem like
wallpaper if we forget where we are.

Beauty is in the eye of the beholder,
But the beholder must remember to look for the
beauty.

It's nice that it's always there though,
In so many different shades.

The joy's yellow, the navy of melancholy;
Poison's purple, hope's green.

I didn't expect three weeks to hold them all as
strongly as it did.

So, Derek (and whoever may be reading),
I wanted to tell you that what you cried about in
the kitchen is true:

It's all here. It's all right here, all of the time -
And you have been blessed with eyes that see
and a heart that feels;
Goosebumps as signal fire and a yearning for the
proper sequence of words.

This is the world you live in,
The only way you can not be here is if you
forget you always are.

I love you,
Very much.
bang

www.ingramcontent.com/pod-product-compliance
Lightning Source LLC
La Vergne TN
LVHW050938200726

843508LV00011B/2381